BLACK N BLUE BOYS / BROKEN MEN

BY DAEL ORLANDERSMITH

★

DRAMATISTS
PLAY SERVICE
INC.

★

BLACK N BLUE BOYS / BROKEN MEN received its world premiere at the Goodman Theatre (Robert Falls, Artistic Director; Roche Schulfer, Executive Director) in Chicago, Illinois, on October 7, 2012. It was directed by Chay Yew; the set design was by Daniel Ostling; the costume design was by Anita Yavich; the lighting design was by Ben Stanton; the sound design was by Mikhail Fiksel; the dramaturg was Tanya Palmer; and the production stage manager was Kimberly Osgood. All roles were performed by Dael Orlandersmith.

SCENES

Mike

Flaco

Larry

Ian

Timmy

Flaco 2

Tenny

Ian 2

Mike 2

NOTES

BLACK N BLUE BOYS / BROKEN MEN can be done by any race/gender and can performed as a solo or multi-character work.

Characters are ALL male. Their ages range from eleven to fifty. Each of them has had a history of abuse.

Stage should be bare except possibly for chairs and a table.

BLACK N BLUE BOYS / BROKEN MEN

MIKE

Narrator moves from cell talking/becoming Mike/once in the spotlight has become Mike/black/thirty-eight/he's worked up/ upset.

I'm a writer AND a social worker / I got my high school Diploma / went to college / I DID THAT / I did not let what my parents did take that away
I got my high school diploma / went to college
I did that
I did NOT let what my parents did take that away from me
I remember this one fight they had … Man this was a HORROR, man / It really was … she had given birth to my baby sister two weeks before / and both of them had been drinking and she and she said *(Does her.)* "I need money"
he gave her money / and she said *(Does her.)* "This ain't enough for seven kids — there's seven kids here" *(Becomes self.)* and he would say *(Does him.)* "Well ALL those motherfuckin kids ain't mine — that baby girl ain't mine — and there's ONE I know for sure ain't mine" *(Voice trails off. Becomes self.)*
and
ANYTIME he said that / He looked at me
(Beat.)
he went outside and was standing on the corner with some other guys / they all had plastic cups and they were passing a bottle around between them in a paper bag and I was about seven and I remember looking out the window / looking at all of these guys but especially him

And

they were all wearing these loud colored suits / these played out popcorn pimp suits / they wore their hats at a rakish angle / and they all got their shoes from Regal Shoes stores / or Florsheims / shiny patent leather shoes or platforms

they're saying shit to all these young women walking past / a lot of the time they don't even talk TO the women / they refer to a body part *(Does a voice.)* "Oh man look at that ass / would love to ride that ass / would love to EAT her all night long"

they would look at the girl and say it while talking to each other as if she were an inanimate object

(Becomes self.)

My mother would look out the window watchin all this and she would say "Motherfucker I'll snatch you out your pants and I'll disconnect that bitch from her asshole"

Then she would sit at the kitchen table holding my baby sister and giving her a bottle and she was drinking and smoking cigarettes with a friend of hers and I said *(As if to her.)* "Mom you shouldn't be smoking / it's not good for the baby and also you've been drinkin — you may drop her" *(Becomes self.)*

And my older brother — he was home and he said *(Does him.)* "Yeah Mom / Mike is right"

(Becomes self.)

And she said *(Does her.)* "Let me tell you two no-good lil NIGGAS something / YOU don't tell me SHIT / you don't tell me a fuckin thing" /

(Becomes self.) then she looks at ME and says "SPECIALLY YOU NIGGA"

I HATE being called that / NIGGER — I HATE IT

They both called us that / NIGGER and they called my Sisters "Nigger Bitches"

(Beat.)

So this day / he was standing on the corner drinkin / she was inside sittin at the table drinkin / fuming / gassin herself up / using what he said about me and my new little sister maybe not being his / I was watching her work herself up / she actually MADE herself breathe heavy / she was prepping herself / giving herself permission to drink more and fight him

She and her friend almost finished a fifth of scotch

It was about one o'clock in the afternoon

She handed my sister to her friend and she went outside with a butcher's knife. She stood at the top of the stoop.

we watched from the window as she yelled at him saying *(Does her.)* "NO GOOD NIGGA BASTARD / YOU THE ONLY NIGGA I BEEN WIT FOR EIGHT YEAR / HOW YOU GONNA SAY THAT BABY GIRL AIN'T YOURS"
(Becomes self.)

He looked up at her and said *(Does him.)* "You need to take yo ass back in the house and stop fucking wit me" *(Becomes self.)*

And she is REALLY breathing heavy now and yells *(Does her.)*
"FUCK YOU / YOU NO-GOOD BLACKASS MOTHER-FUCKER"
(Becomes self.)

She runs down the steps with a butcher's knife / and goes straight for him / Some of the men try to stop her / but she swings the knife in their direction / they back away
(Slight pause.)

They back away laughing

My father goes to grab her / she cuts him across the palm of his right hand / he jerks back and raises his left hand to block her again / he grabs her hand / she breaks loose / she goes to cut him across his torso / he jumps back and kicks her in the stomach / she goes down

He gets on top of her / grabs her by the hair / and slaps her face side to side / she's screaming / screaming her lungs out / some of his friends try to pull him off / but he shoves them back

Then

He bangs her head against the pavement screaming *(Does him.)* "I TOOK YO ASS IN WHEN NOBODY WANTED YOU / ALL THEM KIDS YOU GOT / YOU WAS OUT THERE HOEIN AND ON DOPE / I ACCEPTED THAT TRICK BABY MICHAEL / HOW MANY MEN WOULD DO THAT BITCH"
(Becomes self.)

My older brother looked down at me and said *(Does him.)* "Come on Mike / get away from the window."
(Becomes self.)

Later that night I asked him "What's a trick baby?"

My older brother said *(Does him.)* "It means a baby born from a hoe / the father is one of the men she picks up for money"
(Becomes self.)

And

I asked *(As if to them.)* "is that what I am?"

They all got quiet

My older brother said *(Does him.)* "yeah Mike / that's what you are"
(Back to audience.)

I didn't fully understand what that meant — sex / I didn't know / I
was seven but then again / I DID know

I saw the women standing outside the train station on Junius Street

I knew what they were doing was bad

Therefore

I knew I must ALSO be bad

(Beat.)

But I knew there was MORE

I knew I didn't want to live like this

I KNEW that at SEVEN

I loved to read

I'd tried to stay away from the house as much as I could

I spent lots of time at the library

I would actually be excited to go

By the time I was ten / I read Charles Dickens and I thought "Man,
he lives just like me except he's English."

Those words would hit Me and I could see me and Pip running
down Brooklyn streets hand in hand finding then beating DOWN
my FAKE father and we'd laugh / sidestep / slide past the Artful
Dodger and slap five

Later I read Claude Brown and Piri Tomas and Tasted / smelled /
walked Sal / soul / be bop / hip hop / ditty bop NOISE

Even later

I read Dostoyevsky understanding the need FOR SOMETHING
PURE / understanding the need to kill to make it all PURE

I read them and knew I wasn't alone

I reached for THEM — those writers when I got / slapped / kicked /
punched and called NIGGER from them — my mother and HIM

I reached for them / wondering who my REAL Father was

And

Did he know I existed

I reached for THEM when my two brothers went to jail

I reached for THEM when two of my sisters got hooked on drugs
and when the youngest one got lost in the bottle

I kept REACHING FURTHER

Tolstoy

Baldwin
Morrison
Henry James
When I reached for THEM I was in Brooklyn but I was also
BEYOND Brooklyn / I was BEYOND rat filled tenements and
popcorn pimps and nickel and dime whores and worn down rattling
train stations / I reached for them / kept reaching for them and others /
I kept reaching and reaching and KNEW I was not a NIGGER
TRICK BABY / I was NOBODY'S NIGGER / I was NOT
I was BEYOND
I KNEW I was gonna write about kids like me
I KNEW by writing that it would help kids like me
I KNEW I would NEVER treat a kid the way I was treated
I KNEW
(Beat.)
By the time I was Fifteen / HE had left for good and mother was
NEVER sober and would say *(Does her.)* "ALL that money you
makin / you ain't bringin none in heah / he left me cuz a YOU /
Cuz you wasn't HIS"
(Becomes self.)
I see her / I hear her but I'm BEYOND her
My English teacher helps me with colleges and I get into City
College
I get into a private room at the Dorm
(Slight pause.)
It was like having my own apartment
It was INCREDIBLE
It was my OWN space and I filled it with books
And
Even though I was a full time student and working part time / I still
wrote
I wrote poems/stories about Brooklyn
I dug into those words trying the make the stink of booze come on
to the paper itself
I wanted to use words so the feel of slaps and punches would jump
off the page
I tried to arrange/rearrange those words to picture the man that
planted his seed in my mother
How he did it
I used words to try to imagine him throwing money on that BED

Or

UP against a wall in a Brooklyn hallway

Or

In the backseat of some broken down car in front of the Junius street train station

(Slight pause.)

I became the editor for the school literary magazine *The Promethean* and everyone was taken by the stories

They called me the "NEW Baldwin or the Black Charles Dickens"

(Beat.)

I graduate

The world is OPEN

NOTHING can get in the way

(Beat.)

I get a job in a runaway shelter / I'm doing counseling / I'm doing intakes / I'm also reading my work to the kids / doing writing workshops with the kids and you hear/see how angry they are

You hear it / see it in THEIR words and a lot of the time they take it out on you *(Slight pause.)* ME / they take it out on ME but I understand

I told the Kids about My being a TRICK BABY

And

One of them said *(Does a voice.)* "Yo damn Mike / I got it bad but NOT like you / I'm so sorry man." *(Becomes self.)*

I would read what I wrote to kids in the center and they would say *(Does a voice.)* "Damn Mike / That's just the way the way it is / that's the way I FEEL, man"

(Becomes self.)

I'm sending my work out

I get rejected but keep sending

This goes on for a while

I run writing workshops with the kids and sometimes they can't / don't participate in the workshops because they're too angry / their stays are temporary / some there for a few days / then you never see them again / or someone is put there for a month until they get into a permanent group home / only to run away from that group home after YOU helped get them there

You see the black eyes and swollen faces from their parents

You see the black eyes and swollen faces from pimps / johns

You see swollen arms from shooting drugs

You see teenaged kids who are HIV positive

And or pregnant

You see how bitter beat they are and you know you cannot take it personally and you gotta keep on keeping on

There are days you get totally worn down / out but you gotta keep keeping on

FLACO

Flaco/Nuyorican/aged fifteen, talks to social worker about his past.

You know it's all a hustle to me, yo / know what I sayin / like it's ALL a hustle / I mean / I mean you sit there and you gotta hustle to get me into a group home or whatever / you gotta up my rep / make me look good / not tell people about me being violent cause you gotta place me, *verdad*?
(Beat.)
I mean you know how many group homes I been in, man?
I been in eleven group homes since I was ten years old
My brother has been in seven foster homes
I been in the system for five years
five years, man! And I'm only fifteen.
YOU SOCIAL WORKERS AND COUNSELORS said that you were gonna help
That you were gonna get me out but you and all of you ended up lyin
Lyin like you always do
You lie 'cause you hustle
You gotta make that trick
You gotta PIMP ME
You PIMP me to make YOU look good
You gotta sell me to the system
You gotta Lie and tell them I'm good so you can get me placed / get the Money to get me a place / lessen your case load / so you can go home and get some rest
YOU gotta sell that that lie — ME — / I'm the LIE and you gotta smile while doing it
You gotta know who that trick is real fast and how to tap that trick and keep smiling
You GOTTA be social
Me and you — We're BOTH social workers, man
Gotta turn that trick baby
Maybe I'm telling you the truth or maybe I'm lyin

Layin down my Hustle
(Beat.)
Look at you
Look at you lookin at me
(Moves in closer.)
You like what you see?
Like what you see *mi amor*?
You want me
Me quiere?
quiere mi culo?
(The social worker tells Flaco to stop speaking this way.)
(Slyly.) Okay — awright I'll stop / I promise I'll stop *pero* the look
in your eyes, man made me think — you know?
I mean I KNOW the look
I know the LOOK well
tu sabe?
But I was wrong / so I'll be cool
MAYBE I was wrong / so I'll stop
(Beat. To counselor.)
I really did believe YOU people, man.
I used to believe in PEOPLE
I really did, man
I was stupid for believing adults in general, man because ALL OF
YOU LIE. All this *(Does a voice.)* I PROMISE YOU IT WILL BE
FINE shit yall say. All o yall are a buncha bitches, man and I don't
care if you don't like me callin you that, man
I used to believe in family.
I mean bein there in that house, man with her — My mother, man
and my Pops — Man that shit was fucked up and everybody knew
that it was fucked up. Poppy would get into his Chivas talking
about Puerto Rico and how one day we're gonna leave Coney Island
and get out the projects and see San Juan.
He'd say *(Does him.)* "*La playa aqui hijos* — it ain't real / this Coney
Island beach — it ain't real / the water in PR is PURE/CLEAN"
(Becomes self.)
Then he would take me and my brother Marco under each arm and
bring us to the window and he'd say *(Does him.)* "Take a look at the
water out there but don't see it as Coney Island — See it as Puerto
Rico / if you really look / if you REALLY look PAST it / you can
see San Juan / Santurce."

(Becomes self.)

And me and my little Brother Marco — we would look / squint our eyes and say *(Does this.)* "Yeah Poppy I see Santurce / I RE-ALLY see it / when we goin Poppy / when you gonna take us!" And he always said *(Does him.)* "Soon *hijo* / soon" *(Becomes self.)* My mother — she would say *(Does her.)* "why you telling them that! *Coño* you can't even get enough money together to take the fucking subway!" *(Becomes self.)* and Poppy would say *(Does him.)* "Baby don't talk like that You gotta believe in me babe" and she would say *(Does her.)* "I used to / I used to and Nuthin changed / Nuthin" *(Becomes self.)* his head would drop / he couldn't take her being mean to him / he loved her — my Moms — he really did.

She would get violent sometimes and just for no reason jump on him / then scratch his face or she would grab a knife and one time she did cut him you know? and he forgave her, man.

I mean FORGAVE her for doin that man

made excuses for her all the time *(Does father.)* "Hey Mommy's fiery you know / real fiery"

(Beat.)

He tried to get me and Marco to get close to her / Marco — he REALLY tried *pero* it didn't work and Marco would cry and say *(Does him.)* "Mommy please don't push me away / I love you" *(Becomes self.)* and she would push him away and she would scream and scream

She would tell us *(Does this.)* "I HATE YOU I HATE YOU and they're telling me that I should kill you!" *(Becomes self.)* and we would get scared and say *(As if to her.)* "Who Mommy? who's telling you to kill us?" *(Back to audience.)* and she would say *(Does her.)* "the Daisy Chain People tell me / they tell me that you and Marco keep me from them / they want to hold me / kiss me / make me feel good / they say you and Marco take time away from me so I should kill you both"

(Becomes self/pause.)

I was ten and Marco was six when she started doing this and by the time Poppy came home from work — she'd be okay / I tried to ask Poppy about the Daisy Chain People and he would look at me and say *(Does him.)* "Oh no! Mommy's being fiery again — lissen to Poppa / I'll take care of her" *(Back to being self.)* But I could tell the way he looked that he KNEW / He KNEW Mommy was sick.

He didn't want to see it / he loved her that much

(Beat.)
Poppy was a super in a school and he would get up to get us dressed / give us breakfast and get us to school and when he got out of his job he would come and pick us up
I heard him tell my aunt — his sister that Mommy Needed looking after. Again she was always actin weird / talking to people that weren't there but there were times she could control it / YOU social workers / counselors whatever you call yourselves say it's *(Sarcastically.)* "part of her sickness" BUT I KNOW there were times she coulda controlled that shit / I fuckin KNOW *(Beat.)* So yeah Poppy was doing EVERYTHING. Getting us up for school / cooking dinner when he got home.
This one day after school I had made me and Marco a sandwich and I was watchin TV and Marco was sleepin and I heard her talking to the people that only she saw and heard and then she yelled at me *(Does her.)* "Flaco get out here NOW"
So I go the living room man and she's looking at me and her eyes are bulgin and she got this real long knife and she says *(Does her.)* "The Daisy Chain King — he's my REAL husband / he's telling me to Kill you" *(Becomes self.)* and I say "No Mommy PLEASE / PLEASE Mommy" and I say *(As if to her.)* "Tell him — Tell the Daisy Chain King I'm not a bad boy" *(Looks away.)* so she comes towards me holding the knife and I'm scared shit, man and then she traces the knife over my face / neck / my stomach / back again to my face / neck / she does this a few times *(Pause.)* Then she says *(Does her.)* "pull down your pants" *(Becomes self.)* and I take them down *(Pause.)* Then she says *(Does her.)* "take off your underwear" *(Becomes self.)* So I take off my underwear she touches my thing sayin *(Does her.)* "The Daisy Chain King says I can touch YOU / I can use YOU to get ready for HIM / for the day I become Daisy Chain Queen"

(Pause.)
And I got hard

I got real hard and I said *(As if to her.)* "Mommy stop / please STOP / I don't like this"
(Looks away.)
I didn't like IT but part of me DID
Part of me loved IT
Part of me wanted IT so BAD
I hated that I wanted IT
I couldn't control IT

And she said *(Does her.)* "you want me to stop but you getting hard" *(Becomes self.)* and she laughs / she laughs at me
It happened for like three months
I didn't tell Poppy
I didn't know How to tell him
This One day / she got naked and made me get on top of her …
(Voice trails off.)
I told Poppy and he looked at me
Then
He said *(Does him.)* "Flaco / she didn't touch you LIKE THAT / she's YOUR MOTHER Flaco" *(Becomes self.)* and I say *(As if to him.)* "Poppy she DID / she's SICK Poppy / everybody around the projects says / she don't never leave the house" *(Back to audience.)* and again he says *(Does him.)* "SHE IS YOUR MOTHER Flaco / she did NOT do that / MEN are the ones that touch kids nasty / Women give birth / they don't do that / Your mother / *Mi esposa* didn't do that / STOP it"
(Becomes self/beat.)
One day she was standin by the elevator and there was this kid on my floor / he was twelve and he was waiting for the elevator to go downstairs and she was only wearing a nightgown / she lifted the nightgown and told him to touch her
He ran inside and his Moms came out and beat her and next thing you know all these women jumped on her and they ALL were hittin her
I tried to stop it but I couldn't
I ran to Tee Tee's house and she called the police and Poppy
The ambulance and police came and Mommy was smiling / she kept saying *(Does her.)* "The King loves me / he loves me / he's more than

the Daisy Chain King / he's a God / He's GOD / GOD loves me"
(Back to being self.)
By now We were all outside and people was pointing / looking and laughing
Poppy went inside and got her coat
Marco had me by hand and was crying
A cop — he seemed real nice / he came over to me and said *(Does him.)* "Flaco / what happened?"
(Becomes self.)
And I told him what she did and Poppy heard me
He came over screaming / he said *(Does him.)* "YOUR MOTHER DIDN'T TOUCH YOU LIKE THAT / HOW CAN YOU SAY THAT ABOUT YOUR OWN MOTHER / MY WIFE"
(Becomes self.)
And I said *(As if to him.)* "POPPY SHE NEEDS HELP / SHE DID TOUCH ME LIKE THAT / LOOK WHAT SHE DID WITH THE KID IN OUR BUILDING / MAYBE SHE WOULD HAVE GOTTEN MARCO"
(Speaks outwardly.)
And AGAIN he said "YOU MADE THEM TAKE HER FROM ME / I WAS GONNA GET US TO PR / SHE DID NOT TOUCH YOU OR THAT BOY / SHE GETS EMOTIONAL / THAT'S ALL / SHE'S FIERY BUT NOT LIKE THAT / NOT LIKE THAT WE CAN'T GO TO PR BECAUSE OF YOU"
(Beat.)
The next day / I'm sittin in a Shrink's office — this woman and she's asking me all these questions. Wearing a whole lotta makeup and perfume / you could tell she was *una vieja pero* she was still trying to be young.
She just kept looking at me
She got to the part about Mommy touchin me
I mean I COULD see the look in her face when she got to THAT part / I could SEE how she was tryin NOT to be shocked and she FINALLY said *(Does her.)* "Flaco / it says here your mother touched you but I think the way it's written — there MUST be a mistake"
(Becomes self.) and THEN I DO decide to talk and say *(As if to her.)* "WHY? ... why would that be a mistake" *(Back to audience.)* and she says *(Does her.)* "It says MOLESTATION here" *(Back to being self.)* and I say "what's that" *(Back to audience.)* and she says *(Does her.)* "Well that is what MEN do to girls/women or young

boys" *(Becomes self.)* and I say *(As if to her.)* "You mean like putting their dicks in them" *(Back to audience.)* and she says *(Does her.)* "Yes / that's exactly what I mean" *(Becomes self.)* and I say *(As if to her.)* "Well My Moms ain't got no dick but yeah she touched me like that" *(Back to audience.)* and she says *(Does her.)* "I'm sure you mistook how she touched you / I'm NOT saying that she didn't touch you but women / MOTHERS don't touch their children like this" *(Becomes self.)*

So molestation is what men to do boys or girls

And I told her — this bitch this and of course because she was a woman / She got REAL mad at ME and it was like she wanted to RUMBLE with me, man and she kept saying *(Does her.)* "Flaco / you are VERY young / you can misinterpret things" *(Back to being self.)* and I tell her *(As if to her.)* "I KNOW I'm a kid but I'm telling you the truth / She may be my mother but she did DO that"

I started screaming

I ran around the office screaming

People were trying to grab me and finally someone did

(Pause.)

They bring me to hospital and I'm fighting the doctor and then next you know / all these nurses and people are trying to hold me down

All these faces

All these adult faces

All of them dressed in white

And then all of them HELD ME down

I felt something sting

A needle goes into my arm

Then everything went black

(Beat.)

Then I get sent to the first of the eleven group homes I end up runnin from, man.

LARRY

Larry/who's white/early sixties/he's originally from Brooklyn/ he's sweeping leaves in Central Park/as he works he's also watching a group of men and their sons play touch football/ there's sound of people playing in the park.

Jeesus some of the stuff ya find / unbelievable — / you wouldn't believe the things people do / stuff I find / jeezus people are so nasty / and the stuff ya see /

Like people havin sex in the OPEN / goin to the bathroom in the OPEN — nasty — excuse my language — nasty bastards … there are also people who live here / camp out here / homeless and some of em are nice and I kinda turn my back you know — don't tell anybody cause some of em are good people who are just down on their luck … Central Park is so beautyful

Why do people wanna make it ugly / it's a great park *(He suddenly looks towards the field.)* Whoa — look at that kid run / he can really run / he's got it! / he's really got it this time

TOUCHDOWN! — way to go!

WOW! Now I tell ya / THAT was something!

So the kid got the touchdown

He FINALLY got it

He was workin so HARD to make it

(Sweeps a little but still looking towards the field. Stops sweeping.)

Ya know that kid / his older brother and father come here every Saturday and play football / they been comin — jeez I don't know — what like four years?

Oh I see all kinds of people / I notice the people that come into the Park

Some I know by name / others by sight

And you know a lot of them know me too

Some people call me the Mayor of Central Park / they say *(Does a voice.)* "Hey Mayor Larry!"

People can be real nice

BUT

a lotta time people don't notice me but that's okay
(He looks at the boy again.)
Like this kid NOW — well he's a young man now / He don't know me
(He shakes his head.)
That Father and older brother of his — they always ran him Hard,
Ya know?

I'm lookin at this guy and can tell he went to some Ivy League school and he's some kinda lawyer / stockbroker type and his wife runs up his charge card
I see him joggin a lot too
The father — he's not young but he thinks by all that joggin he does it's gonna keep him young
I see him tryin to pick up young girls on the Joggers' trail
And
I see the girls exchange looks and laugh at him behind his back
The young girls call him "CHICKEN NECK"
You know how as you get older / the skin around your throat sags? Well this guy has a saggy neck
If he ever says somethin to me nasty that's what I'll call him / I'll say, "SCREW YOU CHICKEN NECK" / but again why would he notice a guy like me?
He's arrogant that guy — so full of himself
(Picks up the broom and swings it a little.)
I'd like to hit him with this …
(Beat.)
You know four years ago is when I first noticed them
I remember seein a whole bunch of them — friends of the father and their wives and kids and they All seemed to be having a good time / and I was trimming some hedges and I looked over and saw the younger son turning rope for some girls playin double dutch / and the women were sittin under this tree talking / sunbathin / eatin and All the guys — except for the young guy were on the field playin Frisbee and softball …
Next you thing you know / This SCREAM comes from center field and the father comes runnin towards the Younger son and when he gets to him / he yanks the rope out his hands and says *(Does him.)* "NO / THIS GAME IS FOR GIRLS / UNDERSTAND / YOU

DON'T PLAY THIS / GET ON THE FIELD NOW!"
(Becomes self.)
I mean this guy was REALLY pissed off about this — Really
And even the other guys were telling him that it was no big deal
and — this woman / I guess it mighta been the wife said *(Does her.)*
"Oh come on — you're overreactin"
(Becomes self.)
This guy just looked at her and said *(Does him.)* "Look he's A MAN /
maybe I'm old-fashioned — too bad / He needs to act like a MAN
and I'm gonna see that he does."

So
Yeah after that / I would see them on the field a lot on Saturdays
The father and the older Brother would throw footballs as hard as
they could knocking the poor kid down / they'd toss Frisbees as
high and fast as they could makin the kid run
(Becomes self.)
I never really saw that kid enjoy himself
I mean when you come to Central Park it's supposed to be fun
For FOUR years / they pushed and shoved and bullied that kid
Many times they'd do in front of the other guys / I'd hear the father
say to the older son *(Does him.)* "you and ME will MAKE him into
a man / I CAN'T BE EMBARRASSED"
(Becomes self/increduloulsy.)
HE can't be embarrassed huh?
Jeezus / — excuse my language what an asshole
What a real asshole
And the older brother is an asshole too
How could he treat his Own brother like that?
The stuff this guy is teachin his sons …
just 'cause someone has a kid — it don't make them a parent — ya
know?
(Sweeps again.)
Well that kid — he showed em today
He really showed em
Man — it was Great! TOUCHDOWN
He made a TOUCHDOWN
I guess they made him a "MAN"

IAN

Ian — late thirties/A 2000s-era rock song plays as a loop. *

Nothing can hold you back. Nothing can get in your way except for you.

Look at me I come from three generations of Irish / Scottish drunken pint glass Philosophers whose only function was to get and stay pissed and give their ninety proof advice while falling off of a pub stool …

Then

They staggered Home / beat their wives and kids

Passed out

Hungover of course the next morning — apologetic — the next morning / can't remember the night before and begging forgiveness only to do it again

My father, my Da is of that lineage

Sitting in the pub talking about how great the '60s were / how great a singer he was / IS / how he *(Sarcastically.)* ALMOST Made it to AMERICA

He got from Belfast to Manchester or — Madchester as We call it and no further

And when he gets in it — the whiskey / there's no turning back / and when he's in it there's no telling what's going to happen or how it will *(Does father.)* "talk to me / make me do things / say things that I don't mean" *(Back to being self.)* It — the whiskey may soften him / make him nostalgic / or he may become belligerent

the stories and the reactions are ALWAYS completely different EACH time / he gets in the pub then comes the stories about meeting John Lennon and how John heard him play and said to him *(Does him.)* "Join us / be the fifth Beatle / We're going on tour in the States"

or maybe it was Van Morrison who wanted him to go on tour to the States or maybe Wilson Pickett wanted him to be in his band and called him his "Irish Soul Brother" and EVERYONE in the pub is enthralled

---

* See Special Note on Songs and Recordings on copyright page.

(Becomes self.)
Sometimes he made me go with him to the pub because he KNEW
he would get pissed and needed someone to get him home and that
someone had to be ME / During the week / he drank less / would
have a few pints which is why he thought he wasn't a drunk *(Does his
voice.)* "I fuckin work / NEVER miss work / Yew've food in Yew / I
pay for the flat / clothes are on yer back / I'm entitled to a bit o fun /
to hell with youse" *(Becomes self.)*
then of course he gets home LATE yelling at Mum / Beating Mum
because the food is cold *(Slight pause.)* He'd beat me too
(Beat.)
I was raised in the Council flats and Saturday night and the council
Flats — I mean it can get mad / REALLY mad? All these drunk
adults and they're fighting / pissed out of their skulls because it's
Saturday night and they can't go anywhere because there's no
money / and they can't do anything because there's no money and
that's the one night that's built up in songs and movies / where all
the promises are made / you fall in love on Saturday night / you
dance it ALL away on Saturday night / the whole week is geared
towards Saturday night / nothing matters except Saturday night /
but you're Still in the Council Flat Saturday night and that can't be
sung or drunk away
There was this one Saturday night / Da was in the pub from mid day
to closing / the barman called to say that Da needed *(Sarcastically.)*
"looking after and can't make it back by himself." *(Becomes self.)* It
was cold that night / I mean "freeze-your-bollocks" kind of cold? and
I told Mum / I said *(As if to her.)* "Mum it's cold / Don't want to go"
(Back to audience.) and she says *(Does her.)* "Ian — he's yer Da" *(Self/
back to audience.)* Mum kept after me but I did NOT go to the pub.
(Beat.)
So we're waiting for Da and we're scared out of our wits — especially
me because I refused to get him and we hear him before we lay eyes
on him / we hear him singing "Dead End Street" by the Kinks and
we look out the window and he can barely stand / a mate of his has
walked him home
As I look out the window / I'm petrified / — I KNOW I'm going to
get it and as his mate is trying to get Da up the stairs / I'm watching
by the curtain praying Da would just pass out when he got inside.
I'm listening to his walk that long short unsteady walk
His mate gets him in the flat

Da looks down at me and says *(Does him.)* "Yew lil cunt / Yew didn't come fer me" *(Becomes self. Back to audience.)* he yanks me up and proceeds to slap me about / Mum jumps in / with one hand he slaps her down to the floor
Then
Da throws open the door and drags me outside / holds me over the landing by the collar and I'm screaming / BLOODY SCREAMING / WAILING and some people come out of their flats and they're saying *(Does a voice.)* "NO Mate / put the child down Mate / don't."
(Becomes self.)
And
By now / almost EVERYBODY has come out of their flats and some are looking up and others down and Da is STILL holding me but NOW he is taking in ALL the people around him. He's holding me and taking them ALL in
A smile comes over his face
All these people have become his audience and he's smiling and holding me up to the crowd now / he's actually holding me up / as if I were on display and he's really smiling now and he says / announces to the crowd *(Does him.)* "I'm his DA / he didn't lissen to me / Yer kids have to lissen to yew / if yew have to give them a kicking / give them a kicking"
(Becomes self.)
Then he says to me *(Becomes him.)* "SAY YER NUTTIN" *(Becomes self.)* and I say "NO! NO I WON'T!" *(Becomes himself.)*

One bloke says *(Does voice.)* "Okay mate / you're right / you gotta discipline — you're right but you're bein a bit rough now Mate/ I mean he's little."
(Becomes self.)
And Da says to this man *(Becomes him.)* "NO! In Ireland we KNEW to mind our parents / WE KNEW / people here in ENGLAND KNOW NUTTIN of discipline — NUTTIN / We may be in this God forsaken SHITE country but he will mind ME / and I Will MAKE him mind me / If I have to Kick him all night long / he WILL MIND ME / I AM THE MAN IN MY HOUSE / HE TINKS HE KNOWS IT ALL BUT HE IS STUPID"
(Becomes self.)

He keeps calling me Stupid
And all these kids were crying / beggin their parents to do something
It was like they were also crying for themselves
(Beat.)
And Da by now is thinking he is IT / ALL eyes were on him NOW/
he is a STAR and I finally break down and say "I'm NUTTIN DA /
NUTTIN / I'M NUTTIN!"
And he says *(Does him.)* "WHAT WAS THAT STUPID? WANT
TO MAKE SURE I HEARD YEW RIGHT STUPID? / SAY IT
SO EVERYONE CAN HEAR YEW?"
(Becomes self.)
And I say it again *(As if to father.)* "I'M NUTTIN DA / NUTTIN"
(Back to audience.)
And
He says calmly / so fucking calmly *(Does him.)* "That's right yer
NUTTIN and don't yew ever forget that"
(Becomes self.)
Da drops me
He drops me from the second landing stairwell to the first
I crash onto the first stairwell
Mum rushes past Da to me and some neighbors come as well
The other kids and ME were screaming
ALL OF US KIDS were screaming
I heard one kid tell his Dad *(Does a voice.)* "Why didn't you stop
that man Dad / WHY?"
And
The Dad said *(Does him.)* "Shut it / it has nuthin to do with us"
Everyone goes back inside
Da goes to the fridge and gets a lager / then goes to the sitting
room / drinks it and passes out while sitting in his chair
(Slight pause.)
He sleeps there the whole night
When he wakes up the next morning / SUNDAY morning — it's
all quiet, right? The people who fought last night and drank last
night — they're either sleeping it off or going to church to absolve
themselves —
It's an act of contrition.
They're going to church to give themselves permission to get pissed
and fight the following week.
Because it WILL happen again and does happen every week

Friday and Saturday
Drinking / fighting
Sunday
feeling guilty about drinking and fighting and then going to the priest for absolution
(Slight pause.)
But
THIS Sunday Da didn't go cos he was too hung over. Mum took me to Mass and when we got back / He took one look at my face — the left side was swollen and he then looked down and closed his eyes. He knew it was the WORST beating he ever gave me / Mum told him what he'd done / he couldn't remember all of it — or so he said and he then — goes to reach for me and I scream *(As if to him.)* "DON'T TOUCH ME / I HATE YOU!"
THEN
He went to Mum and she pulled away from him sayin *(Does her.)* "Serves yew right"
He goes into the sitting room and collapses into his chair and he's sobbing / sobbing his fuckin eyes out
Mum is looking at him saying *(Does her.)* "I should fucking leave yew / should take Ian and fuckin leave yew / yew no good bastard yew" *(Becomes self.)* and Da is begging Mum / begging her not to leave / so he crawls across the floor to Mum and he grabs her around the waist and he is NOW WAILIN *(Does him.)* "PLEASE don't leave me / PLEASE / won't do it again Luv / please / love yew / love Ian / PLEASE / I would kill meself if youse left me"
(Becomes self.)
Mum doesn't hug him but she doesn't push him away either

(Back to audience.)
Then Mum held him and Da he's kissing Mum
and he and Mum go into their room and they close the door …
(Voice trails off. Beat.)

I made a decision
I decided that I would no longer cry

I wouldn't cry in front of HIM .
And
I would stay out if I felt like it
So
I did
I would stay out and he would beat me and I wouldn't cry / He got
SO angry — / and he even said *(Does him.)* "Yer a hard stupid bastard
are yew?" And I said *(As if to him.)* "Go ahead Da or I can get the
belt if you like / You do what you need to." *(Back to audience.)* and
he just looked at me
(Beat.)
By the time I was fourteen /
I KNEW I had to get OUT
Get away from Him AND Mum
Away from the Flats
(Beat.)
I stayed to myself
I went to school / I came home studied
I got a part time job
A couple of the boys around the flats tried to Start a row
I fought back
No one bothered me afterwards
In the flats — you HAVE to prove yourself
I also made an effort to lose my accent
I would watch telly and listen to how people spoke
I would borrow tapes from the library
(Becomes self.)
And
alcohol was OUT
I would NOT ever do that
NEVER
I was REPULSED by it
Worse than that —
Disgusted — I was disgusted by it
(Beat.)
Da would look at me and sneer *(Does him.)* "Not a bit of Celt in
Yew / You're a real ENGLISHman / wit all yer schoolin yer still
STUPID"
(Pause.)
By the time I was eighteen / I had enough

I had gotten through school
I decide to go to London and Mum is beggin me not to go and Da
is sayin *(Does him.)* "He up and leaves His Mam and does not care
a shite about me / selfish Yew are / fuckin selfish."
(Becomes self.)
So the day I leave / Da is drunk — it was a Saturday so he started
getting pissed midday and I packed all my gear and Mum had
whiskey in her too and was well pissed / she said she needed it to
(Mocks her.) "Cheer her," *(Becomes self.)* Mum is hugging me and
crying and I can't stand it — the smell of the whiskey IN HER /
her skin clammy / I can't stand HER — the STENCH of HER / Da
says *(Does him.)* "Give us the key / yer no longer welcome here /
don't come back"
(Becomes self.)
And I take the key and throw it in his face and it cuts across his eye
He gets up / as if to hit me
I look back at him smiling but my eyes were hard
I made my eyes so hard
He backed down
(Moves to another part of the stage/A classic Punk song comes up. *)
And then I get to London
I work in a posh restaurant on the west end
I watch/listen to the customers that talk down to me but I bide
my time
I learn about food / wine especially French wine like Latour and
Saint-Émilion
I LEARN
I hang a bit with mates but again mostly stay to myself / attending
University
Studying
ALWAYS studying
(Beat.)
I did it
I got out

TIMMY

1980s. Lights come up on Timmy/aged 11/black. He's smallish for his age/very bright. He's talking to a counselor in a shelter for homeless and runaway kids.

How come I have to live in a group home?
Why?
Why can't I live normal like other kids?
(Voice trails off.)
You know my mother — she always used to say *(Does her.)* "Timmy / it will get better / I promise you / It will" / I believed her and I kept saying *(As if to her.)* "Okay Mom / how can I help you so it can be better?"
Five years ago / we were living in the Bronx — the South Bronx I was six then and the building we lived in — it was okay / there were a lot of drugs / But our apartment was good though. We had a TV and VCR / My Mom cooked and she kept the house clean and she spent a lot of time with me / and she always picked me up from school and she took care of my little sister Tessa.
(Pause.)
Me and Tessa were close — real close *(Beat.)* Me and Tessa didn't know Our dad *(Tensely.)* Mom said he had another family on Long Island … *(Voice trails off. Beat.)*
There were times when she got drunk and passed out and couldn't get up to make dinner so I would go in her bag and get money and buy pizza for me and Tessa
Or
Me and Tessa would have to eat cold cereal for breakfast 'cause she couldn't get up and I had to help her. There were times when she had vomited on herself and peed herself and I would try to help her clean herself up
(Voice trails off.)
She started seeing this man named Roy
He was nice
He would buy food for us and sometimes he would cook for us and

I heard him tell Mom that she should stop drinking because she had to take care of me and Tessa

Roy would take me to school sometimes and help me with my homework and Tessa loved him and called him "Daddy"

He moved in with us and Mom did stop drinking and he would take us to City Island and Coney Island and he was home with us a lot

(Beat.)

When I turned seven / Roy had a birthday party for me and it was a lot of fun *(Slight pause.)* then things started to change

People would come over and they would fall asleep a lot

They would go into the bathroom and come out real sleepy

They would light a cigarette / nod / and hold their cigarette real close to the chair as they nodded and then / they'd jerk up from nodding *(Slight pause.)*

Mom started doing that too

She started going into the bathroom / and then she'd come out and nod

She started doing it a lot and so did Roy

(Beat.)

The house started getting real messy and there were always all these people and people were stealing stuff

Also she started to sell the food stamps. *(Beat.)* there was a boy in school and he said *(Does him.)* "My Mom said that your Mom is a no good junkie" *(Becomes self.)* I hit that boy for saying that *(Beat.)*

THEN

All these men came looking for her and she would take them in her room and they gave her money *(Voice trails off.)*

I was seven and even though I didn't understand everything she was doing / I knew what she was doing was wrong

Tessa didn't understand / she was a baby and she saw things and imitated them. Like one time we were in the living room and I was playing with her and she said *(Does her.)* "Look Timmy / let's play this" *(Becomes self.)* She sticks out her arm and imitates putting a needle in her arm and then pretends to nod.

Mom saw her do that

THEN Mom got into a detox program and she and Roy broke up for good and she was doing good / real good / and me her and Tessa would laugh — man, we would laugh so much / she would tickle us / kiss us ...

I always said *(As if to her.)* "let me know how I can help you to stay clean / I'll do whatever I can."
(Beat.)

Mom *would always promise* to STAY clean and she would for a while / but then she would start again / and there was always a new boyfriend and there were always the men she took in her bedroom *(Pause/beat.)*
I'll never forget — you know THAT day. *(Pause/beat.)* Mom and another new boyfriend — his name was Johnny and they were in her room / they had a needle on the night table in a glass of water and you could see the blood in the water floating around in it.
I heard Johnny say that it was his birthday and I heard Mom say *(Does her.)* "We gotta get some extra stuff so we can party" *(Becomes self.)* then they went out and came back and went straight to Mom's room and they didn't even close the door / I could look from me and Tessa's room into their room / I ALWAYS TRIED to keep Tessa from seeing that but I couldn't ALWAYS … / THAT day I put her in the living room and surrounded her with toys and put the TV on / *(Slight pause.)* But I ALWAYS watched / I watched Johnny — he took the needle out of the bloody water / Mom got a tie / tied his arm / then she tied her arm / took the dope / put it on spoon / she put some of the bloody water on the spoon / lit a match / put the fire underneath the spoon / she cooked the stuff up / she shot him up first / then she drew the blood up into the needle / took a drink of gin / then shot herself up
She and Johnny put on some music / some real old stuff / like 1950s stuff / and they laid down on her bed / I was in bed watching them and this music — it was sad / A Black lady with a pony tail and she had a weird voice / Mom had a whole bunch of her records / she was singing something about "My man" / anyway the music — it made me fall asleep
Then
I woke up to Mom screaming / The screams came from the living room / I ran to the living room / she was holding Tessa / Tessa wasn't moving / Mom kept screaming / just screaming Johnny called 911 / took the rest of the dope and left — he just left *(Pause/*

beat.) What happened was Tessa went into their room / and saw one of bags of dope opened on the night table and ate it
(Beat.)
The police and the ambulance came and one of the ambulance workers REALLY tried to work on Tessa
This ambulance worker — he was this real big guy — he started to cry — this real BIG MAN was CRYING / he kept saying *(Does him.)* "OH MY GOD! / MY GOD! PLEASE NO!"
(Slight pause.)
But
It was too late / Tessa was gone
(Beat.)
Mom — she has supervised visits with me / she's always kissing me / telling me she's sorry about Tessa / saying how she wants me to live with her / she says stupid stuff like *(Mocking.)* "Oh Timmy / you're growing" *(Back to being self.)* and I say "Well yeah I'm eleven / I'm SUPPOSED to grow up right?" I mean I try not to be mean but …
(Voice trails off. Slight pause.)
There are times when I JUST can't LOOK at her
(Beat.)
I really miss Tessa
I think of her ALL the time
I ALWAYS think of that day
(Lights change.)
One day I went into the play room and it was sunny / a real sunny day / and I was thinking how if Tessa was with me / I would have taken her outside so we could play but also I was thinking — more like daydreaming how nice it would be if we lived on Long Island and had a back yard with Mom and our Dad.
(Beat/lights change.)
I went outside and I got on one of the swings
I began to swing really high and I was crying
One of the counselors was watching from inside and yelled out *(Does a voice.)* "Timmy stop swinging so high" and I screamed back *(Does this.)* "No / I want to go high as I can and never come back!" /
(Beat.) One of the girls left her jump rope on the top bar of the swings and I kept trying to get it / I finally did / took the rope / I wrapped it around my neck / and I stood up as I was swinging / hoping the rope would catch the top bar *(Slight pause.)* and I started screaming *(Does this.)* "I WANNA BE WITH TESSA / I WANNA

BE WITH TESSA / I DON'T WANNA BE HERE ANYMORE"
(Speaks normally.) and I kept screaming that / and a whole bunch
of people were outside by now
I just kept going higher and higher
I couldn't get the rope to wrap around the bar but I thought if I
swung real high I'd jump off and then that would be it *(Beat.)*
Somebody called the police and there were these firemen / they
were standing on ladders surrounding me I guess to keep me from
flying off or something / *(Beat.)* I just kept yelling and crying and
then I started laughing / I was laughing So hard but I don't know
why because nothing was funny / but I was laughing / and crying
at the same time and then I stopped laughing and just cried / I
cried so hard that I couldn't see and people kept yelling *(Does this.)*
"Timmy come down / PLEASE come down Timmy" *(Beat. Pause.)*
I slowed down
Then
I just sat on the swing and stopped moving and the swing finally stopped
(Pause.)
I wonder why God is punishing me?
And Sometimes *(Painfully.)* I HATE to say this but sometimes *(Slight
pause.)* I HATE GOD / I KNOW it's wrong but sometimes I do
(Pause/beat.)
I don't really want to die / I just don't want to keep feeling bad all
the time
I mean I'm only eleven
Where's God
I wonder where God is?

FLACO 2

Poppy gets me out of the first of the eleven group homes / Marco was in foster care then and Poppy got him back too

Mommy came home a few days later and she was on medication and things were okay

She cooked but of course Poppy cooked better 'cause he was the one who always did it and you could tell she didn't like doing it

Poppy would come home from work frontin you know?

Sayin shit like *(Does him.)* "the food is SOO good / *Mi esposa* is a great cook / so good to have *mi familia* back / look at your Mommy / isn't she beautiful and PR needs her beauty / When we get offa this stupid Coney Island and get to the REAL Boriqua / people are gonna faint when they see your mother 'cause she's so beautiful / Mommy tell the kids how you told me that I was the ONLY man for you"

(Becomes self.)

Mommy would just look at him saying nothin or she would say *(Does her.)* "I'm going to the Boardwalk" *(Becomes self.)* and she would get up and leave the house

She began to do that A LOT — just GO and then when she did come back — she'd either cry or start hitting again

She began to drink because she thought with medication it would help kill the Daisy Chain voices

So she took the medication and drank and the doctors told her not to but Poppy would say *(Does him.)* "a little Chivas can't hurt" *(Becomes self.)* and of course it DID

She then stopped taking the medication saying "she wasn't crazy" and then started staying in her nightgown again and she began to look at me / Come to me.

I say "no, this needs to stop." And she says "if you don't do what the Daisy Chain King wants I'm telling Poppy you came to me."

And I can't go to another group home. And I don't want to talk to no more bullshit social workers.

And Poppy can't see nothing for what it is. Don't wanna see it.

(Beat.)

And I ain't staying here anymore. I ain't staying. I'll break out man fucking leave here man / fucking leave.

(Pause.)

But I ain't got no money / and I ain't got no place to go / where can I go?

and I just do it to her man, I just do it to her man.

(Beat/speaks outwardly/calmly.)

One day I left school early / I just left man / I didn't feel like being there and I went to Coney with this kid Fernando I know and we went on the Roundup / and the Rollercoaster / He told me *(Does him.)* "Yo Flaco / you could make money / There are some guys around here and all you gotta do is go under the boardwalk and touch their dicks — or they may wanna touch you / but that's it / THAT'S it bro — just TOUCH and they'll give you thirty dollars / and if you feel funny about doin that here in Coney / You could go to the City / You know Forty-nine and Broadway that place PLAYLAND where they have all the pinball games at? / Well I go there / this guy Louie — he's this older guy but he's cool / he's my friend / he sets it up and sends me out / and sent some other kids too but he knows that I ain't no faggot and NONE of us are faggots / He makes SURE that them guys know they can't do nuthin more than what was agreed … it's good money Bro / I mean it feels funny at first / somebody touchin you or somebody's dick in your hand and then their scum in your hand — shit is nasty, man but then you cop the money / wash your hands / and ditty bop on."

(Pause/becomes self.)

I leave Fernando, I think about the money *pero* I ain't no mother fucking faggot.

(Beat.)

One day after school / Me and Mommy are in My room and Poppy finds us and he jumps on ME / He starts hittin ME / callin ME GARBAGE / *(Does him.)* "Get out / Get the fuck out / I'm gonna call that social worker and tell her / tell her you're GARBAGE"

(Back to being self.)

So Poppy is drunk and he calls BCW and two people show up and I hear one of them say *(Does a voice.)* "He's a drunk / The mother is sick and these kids are with them" *(Becomes self.)*

SO they take me AND Marco

Poppy was THEN saying *(Does him.)* "Lissen I made a mistake / Nuthin happened / I made a mistake / PLEASE"

(Becomes self.)

So Poppy called the System played HIMSELF and got played and lost me and Marco for good

So the social worker brings me and Marco to the BCW office and then they Put me in Under 21 for the night / and because of Marco's age they put him someplace else

The social worker said *(Does her.)* "Flaco / you'll stay here for two days until I can get You and Marco into foster care"

What happened was I ended up stayin at Under 21 for a week / A fuckin week

(Beat.)

The social worker told me that because of my age — me being too old / these foster parents wanted Marco but they didn't want me *(Slight pause.)* and also because they had a daughter and they thought I might RAPE HER / they put it in my case folder that I WAS A DANGER SEXUALLY

(Furious.)

In other fucking words — I get called a fuckin RAPIST

Fernando finds out where I am / Poppy told him and he comes down to Under 21 sayin *(Does him.)* "Yo man, that news is all over Coney, man / I hear people talkin about that shit ALL over the Boardwalk *pero* check it out / I know you must be goin through a hard time stayin here / and these kids — Yo they will rip you off / Niggas will steal your drawers / sneakers / hard up mothefuckas, man. Lissen I can call Louie and get you outta here / remember I told you about PLAYLAND? ... Yo it's only a few blocks away from here, man and Louie got a crib where You can crash near here too / you don't have to live in the Shelter, man / think about it B"

(Becomes self.)

I didn't think long / I left with Fernando and thought "I ain't letting nobody take me for free again / I ain't givin it away again / ain't nobody gonna play me again / I'll hustle THEM before they hustle ME"

SO yeah I meet Louie / I go to Playland

(Slight pause.)

So yeah — Playland / Louie *(Sarcastically.)* "HOOKS me up" and says *(Does him.)* "Flaco / I'm gonna buy you some clothes so that way not only will you look good / the trick will know how to spot

you / I'll give you *chabo* to play pinball / he'll come over to you / he'll say who is / he'll mention my name — if he DON'T / say nuthin to him — NUTHIN / if he DOES say my name / you'll know it's cool / let him go to the back FIRST / play a little more pinball for a few minutes / then go to the men's room / it'll take twenny minutes — THAT'S IT Flaco / Fernando will be around / and I'll be outside / so don't worry — we got your back
(Becomes self.)
So this man / old white dude like forty-five comes over / I'm scared / really scared / and he mentions Louie's name and he walks to the back *(Beat.)*
I just wanna run / I just wanna break out / I play pinball / Fernando looks at me to let me know that it's time for me to go the John
I'm walking towards the back and there are all these other kids that are there — these kids my age / and a lot of them are hustling and there are also families playin pinball / just family hangin out
As I walked towards the Back / I wondered if the families knew what was goin on
I get in the john / I go into the Stall
This man — fucking pig, man / fuckin yellow teeth and he got dandruff and it's all over his coat and his skin — his skin is flaky too and he smelled like cigarettes and liquor and he was lookin down at me sayin *(Does him.)* "Oh you are Flaco / you really are / did you know that *flaco* means handsome in Spanish" *(Becomes self.)* and I say "Yeah I know" *(Beat.)* he unzips my pants and puts his hand on my dick, man / and he keeps sayin *(Does him.)* "Flaco you like it / you like it" *(Becomes self.)*

When he finished he said *(Does him.)* "Flaco I wanna see YOU again / JUST you / I'll tell Louie" *(Becomes self.)* then he gives me an extra twenny and winks saying *(Does him.)* "The extra money is our secret" *(Becomes self.)* He walks out of the stall / I hear him run water in the sink / then he leaves
I stay in the stall and I started throwin up

I go to the sink / I WASH

I just kept washing
I can't get clean enough man
(Beat.)

I walk outside
Louie puts his around me and says *(Does him.)* "You did good Flaco /
real good" *(Becomes self.)* and he hands me thirty dollars and of
course I don't tell him about the twenny I got slipped / they take
me back to Louie's crib / I smoke weed for the first time and I drink
some vodka
That was my first time getting high, man
SO yeah I got laid at twelve and then I got high at twelve and
copped my first hustle
(Beat.)

I got tired of Louie taking money
He was givin me and everybody else thirty and he's copping like
three hundred EACH from us / one day I say to him *(As if to him.)*
"Louie, man / you make mad money offa us and we get like only
thirty?"
(Outwardly.)
He hit me
He jumped on top of me and started hittin / the other kids were
scared / and even though they felt the same way / they didn't say shit
Man, I left the crib started turning tricks on my own
I started trickin in the west Village
I'd get a room when I could
I'd sleep in the street or go to shelters and then leave the next day
They would put me in group homes and of course I'd leave them too
I would never let nobody run me again, man
If I got to sell myself, man / I'll be my OWN pimp
(Pause/beat.)
This one night I had a real rough trick
This motherfucker just kept takin me
He just kept takin me from the ass, man
He was big

Not just his dick but HE was a big dude
He said *(Does him.)* "You little Spic / like me in your ass like this /
You Spics like to fuck / You don't like me callin you that / too
fuckin bad / I'm a mean white motherfucker, right?" *(Becomes self.)*
And
I HAD to take it, man
He knew I had to take it 'cause he was so much bigger than me and
plus his driver was in the car
He took me in the back of his limo
The driver had the radio on / was reading the paper
So the john finishes / throws me the money and says *(Does him.)*
"Get the fuck outta my car"
(Back to being self.)
He was this businessman
The kinda nigga who had some pretty wife and kids somewhere on
the upper east side or in Westchester
If I was to tell people how many guys like that come cruising —
people wouldn't believe me
Sometime you get cruised with them and their girlfriends or wives
and you do threesomes
(Beat.)
He throws four hundred dollars at me
I NEVER made that much, man
I went and got a room
I bought some weed / wine
I bought some bandages and stuff
I was bleedin,
I was bleedin bad, man
I was sick man
Sick of all of it, man
Him callin me a Spic
Fucking two years on the street
And him givin me the MOST money I ever made and me doin
nuthin when he called me a Spic
(Beat.)
Getting four hundred dollars / the most I ever made
All for bein a Spic
A no good dirty spic whose first fuck was his own Moms and who
nobody believes
Four hundred dollars for ALL that man

Four hundred dollars to take it up the ass and bleed
Man I just wanted to die, man
I just wanted to be GONE
I mean I had just turned thirteen man ...

TENNY

White/late fifties – early sixties. He is sitting in a jail cell but audience does not realize it at first.

My nephew Sean — God could that kid swim. My brother taught him to swim when he was only a few months old.

I mean he went straight from his Mother's womb to the ocean. My brother laughed and said *(Does him.)* "Hell Sean went from one ocean to another!" …

Do you know by the time Sean was six — he was an expert swimmer? He and his little friends formed a swimming group! I mean these little kids — four little boys met every Saturday and swam! …

He didn't care how cold it was. Here was this six year old who told my brother *(Does him.)* "Dad-I-want-to-swim-and-be-a-professional-swimmer-when-I-grow-up-and-me-and-my-friends-do-too-and-I-know-we-live-in-Sag-Harbor-and-it-gets-cold-but-if-you-and-my-friends'-parents-find-a-place-for-us-to-keep-swimming-we-will-be-famous!"

(Becomes self.)

My brother said he couldn't believe how Sean was so bold and ambitious at six! … neither could any of us and all us would go to watch these kids swim … these funny little boys / these string bean boys take that water / move through it / push it back / embrace it. I mean there was NOTHING they couldn't do in water … nothing They made water THEIRS

They moved their bodies / they OWNED their bodies

these strong / string bean / little boys / little men

(Slight beat.)

I wonder where it came from … not just the swimming but the boldness and the confidence that Sean had. I mean sometimes my Sister-in-law would say to Sean *(Does her.)* "Sean stop showing off" *(Becomes self/angry.)* and he wasn't showing off / He WASN'T / he found something he loved or better yet — what he loved was embedded in him / it was THERE / He was BORN with it …

She — My sister-in-law — has no patience for people who are

different. I mean anything outside of her cramped / silly world does not exist …

I am aware of what is within people and I was aware of Sean and how he would say to me *(Does him.)* "Uncle Tenny I'm NOT showing off Uncle Tenny / I just feel good in water and I feel good when the water touches my skin / what's the matter with feeling good."

And

I'd say to him *(As if speaking to him.)* "There is nothing wrong Sean. NOTHING. Don't listen to ANYONE that puts you down" *(Back to audience.)* and he grabbed me and hugged me and said *(Does him.)* "Thanks Uncle Tenny" *(Becomes self/back to audience.)* He called me Tenny. See my name is actually Terence but when Sean was very little he couldn't say "Terence" — it came out "Tenny" so thus "Uncle Tenny."

He had just come from swimming practice and I was babysitting him

And

He ran to the car / threw the door open and grabbed me saying *(Does him.)* "Uncle Tenny / Uncle Tenny / I'm so happy! Take me for ice cream / PLEASE let's get some ice cream" and I said *(As if to him.)* "Sean you just came from swimming plus it's 28 degrees / aren't you cold?" *(Back to audience.)* and He said *(Does him.)* "I don't care about it being cold Uncle Tenny / I love to swim anytime and I love ice cream anytime." *(Becomes self. Beat.)*

So

We drive to a Dairy Queen and we get ice cream and as I'm driving towards the house / he's telling me about how he knows he's getting stronger *(Does him.)* "Uncle Tenny — you know next year when I turn seven I'm gonna be so much faster! I bet I'll beat all my friends in the team and my backstroke is getting so much stronger Uncle Tenny!" *(Becomes self.)*

His face — it was so animated and ALIVE and then he reaches over and licks my face and I say *(As if to him.)* "Sean what are you doing — I'm driving, man!" *(Back to audience.)* and he says *(Does him.)* "you have leftover ice cream on your face and you had strawberry and I had vanilla and I want to taste the strawberry!" *(Becomes self.)* Then — and I still had one hand on the wheel — I lean over and lick him back and say *(As if to him.)* "That's right and I didn't get any vanilla!"

(Back to audience.)

And

We both laugh and laugh
(Beat.)
I pull over near an open field not far from the house and Sean and I are laughing and he says *(Does him.)* "hey Uncle Tenny put on the 1910 Fruitgum Company" *(Becomes self.)* They were this band — bubblegum band from the '60s and the song was "Yummy Yummy Yummy." He knew it because my sister-in-law always played '60s music …
I made a copy of it 'cause I knew Sean liked it and we're singing
And
I tickle him and then tickle him some more
And as I tickle him / I reach under his shirt
I'm feel the smoothness of his chest
I move to his stomach
Tickle him again
Then
I go back to his chest
I massage his nipples
I begin to massage and pull his nipples
He moans
He moans *(Does this.)* "Uncle Tenny / Oh Uncle Tenny"
And
I reach down
I kiss his nipples / his boy / girl voice moaning "Uncle tenny / uncle tenny"
I keep kissing
Kissing
Licking
Him
He tastes like ice cream and salt and ocean
His skin is OCEAN
Salt
Salt ocean skin and ice cream
(Slight pause.)
I unzip his pants
I touch his penis
And he looks down and says *(Does this.)* "Penis" *(Becomes self.)* but it sounds like "peanuts" and I say *(As if to him.)* "PEANUTS — you mean PENIS" *(Back to audience.)* and he says *(Does him.)* "I said PENIS" *(Back to audience/becomes self.)* and I said *(Back to him.)*

"Sean it sounded like you said PEANUTS" *(Back to audience.)*
And
Again
We laugh
(Pause.)
I turn him over
I kiss his back
I kiss and kiss his back
I lick his back
And
He laughs
(Beat.)
I part his legs
A child DOES have sexual feelings and they KNOW what they feel /
HOW they feel so if a child I find beautiful and who ALSO finds
me beautiful wants to reach for me … How can that be wrong?
It's HUMAN and we should not turn our backs on what is Human

(Beat.)
Again I know for the MOST part that this does NOT always
apply — if the child does not want it, if the adult forces him it is
predatory. I would never do that.
(Pause.)
I get off of Sean
There is blood
I try to wipe away the blood
He pushes me away
He cries
I say *(As if to him.)* "Do you want to go back to the Dairy Queen"
He looks at me and says *(Does him.)* "Take me home."
I drive him home
He sits in the passenger seat rocking back and forth
(Beat.)
I didn't mean to cause him pain
(Beat.)
He runs out of the car / into the house
My sister-in-law and brother are home
I don't drive away

I don't know why
My brother runs to my car
He pulls me out of the car
He punches
Kicks me
I don't fight back
(Beat.)
In court / I plead guilty
Family members look at me like I'm a piece of garbage
People cannot help the way they're born — they can't. I mean there is no prerequisite for genetics and conditioning / so whoever — whatever the powers are that be / who/whatever that is / THAT's where it ALL lays
(Slight pause.)
I fight — I DO fight with myself / I do it all the time / looking at young boys and I HAVE been with a few / and there was that part of me that knew I shouldn't / I tried to fight that THING I was BORN with / I was BORN — made this way by whatever GOD/THING you want to call it
(Pause.)
I can't help it
I cannot help it
(Beat/lights come up and we see that Tenny is in a jail cell.)
When I first got here / people asked what I was in for
I said assault — All I said was assault
Then
One day my lawyer came to see me
And
One of the inmates was on cleaning duty
And
He recognized my lawyer and knew that he specialized in child molestation cases
The others of course found out and I was attacked and taken out of GP — General Population … they stopped calling me Tenny
They call me tenia
And
I guess that's what I am
A Tenia
A Worm
(Lights fade.)

IAN 2

Bass line of a 1970s rock song comes up. *

I needed to get out of London
I was CHOKING
I really felt like I was choking
I wanted MORE
(Slight pause/beat.)
New York
A hustle here, a hustle there. New York City's the place where.
Hey babe, take a walk on the wild side.
New York City's the place INDEED
Places that stayed open 24 hours!
Chatting up all these girls because they love my accent / I had so
many women the first four years I got here
They'd ask me to say words like *(Does American accent.)* "can't" and
then of course I'd say *(British accent.)* "can't" and others words like
"dynasty" / "Anthony" — THEY practically wet themselves
(Beat.)
Here in the States
I continue my studies
I studied day and night
I graduate
I graduate with flying colors
Get a GREEN CARD / work as a clerk for Price Waterhouse but it
pays shit so I work construction on the side, no union, no taxes.
I share a flat in the east village with a bunch of blokes from England /
Ireland / Scotland — if we were back home / we'd have nothing at all
to do with one another
All they did was work / then go to bars every night and SHAG —
or SAY they shagged — that's ALL they did / stinking of whiskey
and lager / telling whiskey lager lies
(Pause/beat.)
I would take these long walks

---

* See Special Note on Songs and Recordings on copyright page.

I would walk from the Village to the upper east side
I would walk fast
Really fast
Then slow
I slowed down as I got to those upper east side blocks
I loved how quiet it was
I would get there and take in ALL the buildings
I would watch people enter the building with DOORMEN
I loved the ease / the sense of KNOWING that a door should be
open to you and WILL be
I saw how people actually walked slower and moved differently
than the people Downtown
I took in how clean the streets were
I would see / STUDY well dressed people
I would look them in the eye
And
As I stared at them I thought, "That's right / SEE ME / I want you
to SEE me / ONE DAY I'll be living HERE"
Then
I'd walk back downtown
I'd walk very slow
I wanted to delay going back
I was so aware of how the streets changed
Or
How the level of noise heightened
As I got closer to the east village / I could smell the smells
Urine
The stench of cigarettes and booze
The smells of cheap food
I'd look at the Council Flats — Housing projects as you say here in
the States and from the open windows or on the streets I'd hear /
see people fighting / crying / pissed or stoned. So I got out of there.
I got a place up in Murray Hill
Got a job at Deloitte as an accountant
I said to myself / "You're not there YET Ian but you're CLOSE"
(Beat.)

THEN

I meet HER — THE ONE
Christmas party at the Firm
She's gorgeous and nice
Comes from Greenwich Connecticut
And
She looked at ME
She didn't look about to see if everyone was looking at her 'cause she
knew she looked good
She looked at ME and smiled
(Beat.)
I couldn't believe she looked at ME
The other blokes in the room were more established than ME
They CAME from money
She looked at ME
(Beat.)
We did great / crazy things
Went to Coney Island at night
She'd have midnight suppers that she cooked and we'd dress up!
It was great
(Beat.)
Sleeping with her — it was fantastic
We'd make love for hours
I told her about Mum and Da
I never felt LIKE this way about anyone
(Beat/almost a whisper.)
I kept thinking about how one day she'd leave
I KNEW one day she would
I wondered if she laughed at things I told her
Or
if she told other people — like her girlfriends about what I told her
about Mum and Da
I HATED that I liked her
(Slight pause.)
One day I said *(As if to her.)* "You know if you ever want call it quits /
or if you want to see other blokes — fine by me"
(Back to audience.)
And she looks at me like I'm Mad and says *(Does her.)* "Ian I'm in
love with YOU"
And
I love hearing that

And
I hate hearing that
(Slight pause.)
I don't know what to do with that
(Beat.)
I never say it back
I buy flowers
I buy perfume
But
I COULDN'T
(Beat.)

I met her family / went to Greenwich and had dinner / the dinner-ware ALONE was more than my rent
(Beat.)
They were very nice her family / very welcoming
Her mother kept refilling my plate
There were jokes / family stories and they made a point to include me
Her parents invited me to come back
And My girlfriend — she smiled
(Beat.)
I felt like I didn't belong
I felt like ANY moment someone would say, "we see through you / you dumb MICK / you're rubbish / YOU'RE stupid / you'll NEVER belong."
(Beat.)
I want her more than ever but I'm now I'm petrified
(Beat.)
We'd be out on the double dates say and maybe we went to dinner and the check would come and I'd say, "let the rich girl from Greenwich pay."
And
She'd feel bad
and couple of times / she got up and walked away
I grabbed her by the arm / pulled her back
I'd grab her and pull with such force it sometimes would leave a mark
(Pause.)

I'd see the black and blue mark on her arm
I couldn't STAND seeing it
I'd feel like shit for doing that
I'd buy her flowers …
(Beat.)
NOW I get promoted to senior accountant / I move to the east sixties
Doormen open / close / hold doors for ME
NEW YORK IS MINE
FINALLY MINE
She talks about us living together
I change the subject
She throws a promotion party for me / surprise party at my place /
everybody from the firm is there / there's loads of food she cooked
and she's looking great / and she kisses me and says *(Does her.)* "Ian
I am so proud of you" *(Becomes self. Beat.)*
There was a girl — secretary — who was there and I was dancing
with her and my girlfriend was dancing with another bloke — it
was a great party / loads of fun
(Beat.)
She got the Saint-Émilion. The wine I had served in the restaurant
in London. I knew it went WELL with crudités.
I know I shouldn't but I HAD to have this wine
I broke my own rule
I had two glasses of wine
I got pissed on those two glasses
I go to the loo / I'm hot / sweaty / and I throw water on my face /
The girl — the secretary comes in / and next thing you know / I got
her against the sink fucking her / I mean I don't even know HOW /
WHY that happened / and next thing you know my girl comes in
and I look over her and just stare at her and I start to laugh …
(Voice trails off.)
The secretary runs out
My girlfriend says *(Does her.)* "Hurry back / there's a room full of
people"
The rest of the party / she's quiet and pretending to smile / serving
people
The party ends
Now it's just me and her and she says to me *(Does her.)* "Ian —
WHY did you do that / WHY?" *(Becomes self.)* and I say "'Cause
she meant shit to me that's why."

And GOD how I want drop to my knees / I want to beg her to forgive me but instead I say "You HATE me now don't you" / And she says "NO / I just don't understand you / I don't"
(Becomes self. Note in his exchange with girlfriend, accent should be an Irish accent.)
I look at her / and I say *(To her.)* "YOU Sit there so holier than thou / I can see you looking at me thinking I'm Shit / YOU thinking you're better than ME MS. GREENWICH CONNECTICUT" *(Back to audience.)* and she says *(Does her.)* "Ian STOP / I'm not thinking that at all / why do you ALWAYS do this"
(Becomes self/some sort of light change happens.)
And I Grab her and I Rave / I fucking RAVE *(As if to her.)*
"Let me tell YOU something Lady / YOU ARE THE ONE THAT IS SHIT / YOU ARE ONE THAT'S NOTHING / YOU ARE NOTHING — DO YOU HEAR ME? — YOU ARE NOTHING / NOT ME!"
And she says *(Does her.)* "WHAT THE FUCK IS THE MATTER WITH YOU! YOU'RE BEING CRAZY / STUPID!"
(Back to audience/quietly.)
I yank her up by her shoulders and shake her and she's crying / I shake her saying "FUCK YEW YOU'RE THE ONE THAT'S NUTTIN / RICH CUNT CALLING ME STOOPID?"
She breaks away from me and tries runs out of the flat …
(Slight pause/music that could possibly come up as a loop is David Bowie's "Repetition."*)
I grab her before she gets to the door / I knock her down / pull her by the collar of her dress and I'm dragging her across the floor and she's screaming / screaming her head off / and I'm kicking her / kicking her as I drag her across the floor
I get her to the window — it's open and I push her torso out / with my knee in her chest and I say *(As if to her.)* "I SHOULD FUCKIN PUSH YOU / I REALLY SHOULD"

"YOU REALLY THINK YOU'RE SOMETHING! — YOU REALLY DO / THERE ARE PRETTIER GIRLS THAN YOU / THERE ARE! / SAY IT / I WANT TO HEAR YOU 'IAN I'M NOT THAT PRETTY'/ SAY IT/ FUCKING SAY IT"

She says *(Does her.)* "IAN I'M NOT THAT PRETTY"

* See Special Note on Songs and Recordings on copyright page.

(Becomes self.)
I say *(As if to her.)* "SAY IT AGAIN"
(To audience.)
AGAIN
She Says *(Does her.)* "IAN I'M NOT THAT PRETTY"

(Becomes self.)
Then I say *(As if to her.)* "THAT'S RIGHT / YOU ARE NOT / and
don't play fucking Martyr with me / You MADE me do this / YOU
DID / So go on leave me 'cause you ALWAYS wanted to anyway / I
KNEW YOU WOULD — GO ON — GET FUCKING OUT!"
(Back to audience.)
She runs past me and leaves
(Long beat.)
I break up the flat after that / I just tear it apart / I remember doing
it but as I was doing it / it wasn't real / it was like a part of me was
standing outside watching

When I woke up the next morning / I was lying in the center of the
sitting room still dressed and then when I looked at what I done — the
State of that room and then I thought about what I did to HER …
(Beat.)
I left messages
I send candy / perfume / she sends them back
On the cards I wrote "I LOVE YOU"
I did write it on the card
I did write "I LOVE YOU"
(Lights fade on him.)

MIKE 2

In the shelters a lot of the time / your co worker calls in sick and or the cook doesn't show up which means the phones are ringing off the hook / when new kids come on in YOU have to do the intakes for the new kids as well as cook dinner and do individual and group counseling
You have to do ALL this ALONE
(Slight pause.)
TODAY was one of those days
(Beat.)
I got yet ANOTHER rejection letter from a grant
This year I thought I was going to get it
And
I just sit there — gutted
I was just gutted man
(Beat.)
So I get to work today and like I said I'm working the tour alone. I told the kids that I really needed them to behave / I said *(As if to them.)* "Look I'm working alone / Totally alone today / also you know how I keep applying for grants for my writing / well this grant that I was banking on fell through so I really need for you guys to be cool."
(Back to audience.)
There was this one kid who was a little younger than the rest named Jimmy / he's nine as opposed to eleven. The shelter housed kids aged eleven to seventeen. His father brought him in two weeks ago begging us to keep Jimmy because HE was homeless and did not want Jimmy on the streets with him.
Jimmy kept acting up / saying *(Does him.)* "YO mike / where do you get your shoes from man / the 99 cents store? Yo, man I'm a call you '99 cent Mike'"
(Becomes self.)
I kept saying *(As if to him.)* "Jimmy I need for you to behave, man / I really do."
(Back to audience.)
And he would stop for a while and then would keep at ME AGAIN.

Finally I yelled *(As if to him.)* "Goddamnit, you're on restriction for three days / go to your room right NOW!"
(Back to audience.)
He yelled *(Does him.)* "You ain't my father man! / I ain't doin NUTHIN you tell me / look at choo wit your 99 cents clothes / FUCK YOU"
(Back to being self.)
He also bragged how he KNEW we couldn't discharge him from the shelter because of his father and because he was so young
He KEPT saying *(Does him.)* "Yo 99 cent Mike / you can't put me out / YO 99/ which yo 99 cent clothes"
(Back to being self. Beat.)
Finally I said *(As if to him.)* "Jimmy / Man you are really really trying my patience and yeah what I'm going to do is call my supervisor and have them tell your father that you HAVE to go / I'll call Special Services and have them get you and bring them down to the office and out of HERE!"
(Back to audience.)
Then
Jimmy BELLOWS *(Does him.)* "99 CENT MIKE / CAN'T GET A GRANT FOR YOUR STUPID WRITIN / ALL OF US LAUGH AT THAT SHIT / AN YO MOMS BEIN A HOE / YOU A STUPID NIGGA WIT A HOE FOR A MOMS / DAT'S WHAT I'M A CALL YOU / 99 CENT NIGGA TRICK BABY MIKE"
(Pause/becomes self.)
I lock the office door
I grab him
The phone is ringing non stop
The other kids have gotten quiet
I put him across my knee
I spank him
I spank / I yell *(Does this.)* "CALLING ME A NIGGER TRICK BABY / I'M NOBODY'S TRICK BABY / I'M NOBODY'S NIGGER / I'M TIRED OF PEOPLE TREATING ME THIS WAY / I TRY / NO ONE SEES THAT / HOW I TRY / I'M TIRED OF GETTING KNOCKED DOWN / I'M TIRED OF GETTING PASSED OVER / I'M TIRED / NO MORE / NO GODDAMN MORE!"
I keep spanking him
Jimmy is fighting back tears but the pain is too great

He tries to bite my thigh / I yank his head back / get a grip on his neck and spank harder
He screams through clenched teeth
He does not want to give in
But
THE PAIN I'M INFLICTING IS JUST TOO GREAT
Jimmy screams "stop man stop." And I hit harder and harder / I hit until my hand begins to hurt / I push him off my lap
(Pause. Back to audience/speaks normal but shaken.)
I open the office door
Jimmy runs to his room and cries himself to sleep
The other clients hurry to their rooms
I didn't have to make them go to bed like I normally did
They ALL just went
My co worker comes on for the next shift
I tell her what happened
She says *(Does her.)* "Good / he had it comin and remember his father said we could spank him 'cause he can be difficult."
(Becomes self.)
I tell her what went on for the rest of the shift / and hand her the minute book where we kept records of our shift … *(Slight pause.)* of course I did not write that I hit Jimmy / I wrote he acted up …
(Pause/beat/speaking as if almost in a trance.)
Yes his father gave permission to spank but you're NOT supposed to hit / It's WRONG to hit / It's wrong … *(Voice drops.)*
See the thing is I KNOW / I KNOW how kids are / I've worked in a runaway shelter for years / I know how kids will try you / test you … I KNOW this
(Beat.)
I know / as much as anybody KNOWS / I come from the "Hood" / I got my ass kicked by my parents / I SHOULD KNOW
when I sit down with the kids / I ALWAYS tell em "I DID IT / SO CAN YOU" …
I always say *(As if to a kid.)* We are here in BED STUY and I'm from Bed Stuy but you don't have to succumb to the street
But you do succumb because it's all you've known / seen / the slap / punch / kick and the high
the touch / kiss / caress is not real and no one ever showed you more
there was some who did not want to show you more
who wanted to keep you in your place

worse yet / there are many who don't see / can't see / want to see / you
they know your story / they think they know your story
they sum you up in a short glance and walk on by
you're dirty — They're not
you're fat — They're not
you smoke, you drink, you shoot / They don't
Can they smell your stench and realize the STENCH, rejection, is
coming from them?
Did they watch you draw on the crack pipe and fill up on IT,
contempt, in their lungs?
Did they watch you cook up and shoot and feel IT, pity, in their veins?
as you nod in the land of a thousand nods?
And when the cold hits on a coatless night
Did they feel the WIND, apathy, on their skin and shiver?
This is what I wanted to scream on paper
I was gonna help / I was gonna make a change / give them — the
kids — a voice — make a change.
How could I lose my cool like that?
How?

EPILOGUE

See it doesn't have to be ALL be black n blue
You can walk your walk
Walk it well
You can be bop / then side step
Then keep walking
Walking straight
And there IS a woman
A woman that strokes your face and holds you
And the way she does it — holds you
She does it so CLEAN
It's not about dreams of palm trees from Brooklyn windows
Or
one hundred proof shot glass nightmares
It's in the walk
A rearranged walk
Not the walk of a hustler
NOT
"the-READY-poised-panther like-knife-in-your-pocket" kind of walk
It's a walk that has an ease
You ain't sure where you gonna go
BUT
You KNOW you gotta get there
And when you get there you wanna be PURE
And yeah every once in a while — you'll see it — the black n blue
And
The Black n blue will turn that trick and make you wail
And you may fall back
Into tricks
Or back up moves
You feign swagger
Or
Be bop
And
the memory of sore nights
And wasted days hit

But
you remember to dig yourself
Dig your back
And
Straighten that back
So
You walk
You pace that walk
You
go
keep walking
go
straight
keep walking
Gone
Gone
Walk on / keep on walking
Gone
Gold
Gold
There ain't no more black n blue
Go on baby — keep walking
It's gold
Gold
It's ALL gold
(Music plays a little louder, something like Moby's "Beautiful," then fades/lights go down.*)

End of Play

* See Special Note on Songs and Recordings on copyright page.

PROPERTY LIST

Table
Chair
Broom

SOUND EFFECTS

People in a park

NEW PLAYS

★ **MOTHERHOOD OUT LOUD by Leslie Ayvazian, Brooke Berman, David Cale, Jessica Goldberg, Beth Henley, Lameece Issaq, Claire LaZebnik, Lisa Loomer, Michele Lowe, Marco Pennette, Theresa Rebeck, Luanne Rice, Annie Weisman and Cheryl L. West, conceived by Susan R. Rose and Joan Stein.** When entrusting the subject of motherhood to such a dazzling collection of celebrated American writers, what results is a joyous, moving, hilarious, and altogether thrilling theatrical event. "Never fails to strike both the funny bone and the heart." –*BackStage.* "Packed with wisdom, laughter, and plenty of wry surprises." –*TheaterMania.* [1M, 3W] ISBN: 978-0-8222-2589-8

★ **COCK by Mike Bartlett.** When John takes a break from his boyfriend, he accidentally meets the girl of his dreams. Filled with guilt and indecision, he decides there is only one way to straighten this out. "[A] brilliant and blackly hilarious feat of provocation." –*Independent.* "A smart, prickly and rewarding view of sexual and emotional confusion." –*Evening Standard.* [3M, 1W] ISBN: 978-0-8222-2766-3

★ **F. Scott Fitzgerald's THE GREAT GATSBY adapted for the stage by Simon Levy.** Jay Gatsby, a self-made millionaire, passionately pursues the elusive Daisy Buchanan. Nick Carraway, a young newcomer to Long Island, is drawn into their world of obsession, greed and danger. "Levy's combination of narration, dialogue and action delivers most of what is best in the novel." –*Seattle Post-Intelligencer.* "A beautifully crafted interpretation of the 1925 novel which defined the Jazz Age." –*London Free Press.* [5M, 4W] ISBN: 978-0-8222-2727-4

★ **LONELY, I'M NOT by Paul Weitz.** At an age when most people are discovering what they want to do with their lives, Porter has been married and divorced, earned seven figures as a corporate "ninja," and had a nervous breakdown. It's been four years since he's had a job or a date, and he's decided to give life another shot. "Critic's pick!" –*NY Times.* "An enjoyable ride." –*NY Daily News.* [3M, 3W] ISBN: 978-0-8222-2734-2

★ **ASUNCION by Jesse Eisenberg.** Edgar and Vinny are not racist. In fact, Edgar maintains a blog condemning American imperialism, and Vinny is three-quarters into a Ph.D. in Black Studies. When Asuncion becomes their new roommate, the boys have a perfect opportunity to demonstrate how open-minded they truly are. "Mr. Eisenberg writes lively dialogue that strikes plenty of comic sparks." –*NY Times.* "An almost ridiculously enjoyable portrait of slacker trauma among would-be intellectuals." –*Newsday.* [2M, 2W] ISBN: 978-0-8222-2630-7

DRAMATISTS PLAY SERVICE, INC.
440 Park Avenue South, New York, NY 10016 212-683-8960 Fax 212-213-1539
postmaster@dramatists.com www.dramatists.com

NEW PLAYS

★ **THE PICTURE OF DORIAN GRAY by Roberto Aguirre-Sacasa, based on the novel by Oscar Wilde.** Preternaturally handsome Dorian Gray has his portrait painted by his college classmate Basil Hallwood. When their mutual friend Henry Wotton offers to include it in a show, Dorian makes a fateful wish—that his portrait should grow old instead of him—and strikes an unspeakable bargain with the devil. [5M, 2W] ISBN: 978-0-8222-2590-4

★ **THE LYONS by Nicky Silver.** As Ben Lyons lies dying, it becomes clear that he and his wife have been at war for many years, and his impending demise has brought no relief. When they're joined by their children all efforts at a sentimental goodbye to the dying patriarch are soon abandoned. "Hilariously frank, clear-sighted, compassionate and forgiving." –*NY Times*. "Mordant, dark and rich." –*Associated Press*. [3M, 3W] ISBN: 978-0-8222-2659-8

★ **STANDING ON CEREMONY by Mo Gaffney, Jordan Harrison, Moisés Kaufman, Neil LaBute, Wendy MacLeod, José Rivera, Paul Rudnick, and Doug Wright, conceived by Brian Shnipper.** Witty, warm and occasionally wacky, these plays are vows to the blessings of equality, the universal challenges of relationships and the often hilarious power of love. "CEREMONY puts a human face on a hot-button issue and delivers laughter and tears rather than propaganda." –*BackStage*. [3M, 3W] ISBN: 978-0-8222-2654-3

★ **ONE ARM by Moisés Kaufman, based on the short story and screenplay by Tennessee Williams.** Ollie joins the Navy and becomes the lightweight boxing champion of the Pacific Fleet. Soon after, he loses his arm in a car accident, and he turns to hustling to survive. "[A] fast, fierce, brutally beautiful stage adaptation." –*NY Magazine*. "A fascinatingly lurid, provocative and fatalistic piece of theater." –*Variety*. [7M, 1W] ISBN: 978-0-8222-2564-5

★ **AN ILIAD by Lisa Peterson and Denis O'Hare.** A modern-day retelling of Homer's classic. Poetry and humor, the ancient tale of the Trojan War and the modern world collide in this captivating theatrical experience. "Shocking, glorious, primal and deeply satisfying." –*Time Out NY*. "Explosive, altogether breathtaking." –*Chicago Sun-Times*. [1M] ISBN: 978-0-8222-2687-1

★ **THE COLUMNIST by David Auburn.** At the height of the Cold War, Joe Alsop is the nation's most influential journalist, beloved, feared and courted by the Washington world. But as the '60s dawn and America undergoes dizzying change, the intense political dramas Joe is embroiled in become deeply personal as well. "Intensely satisfying." –*Bloomberg News*. [5M, 2W] ISBN: 978-0-8222-2699-4

DRAMATISTS PLAY SERVICE, INC.
440 Park Avenue South, New York, NY 10016 212-683-8960 Fax 212-213-1539
postmaster@dramatists.com www.dramatists.com

NEW PLAYS

★ **BENGAL TIGER AT THE BAGHDAD ZOO by Rajiv Joseph.** The lives of two American Marines and an Iraqi translator are forever changed by an encounter with a quick-witted tiger who haunts the streets of war-torn Baghdad. "[A] boldly imagined, harrowing and surprisingly funny drama." –*NY Times.* "Tragic yet darkly comic and highly imaginative." –*CurtainUp.* [5M, 2W] ISBN: 978-0-8222-2565-2

★ **THE PITMEN PAINTERS by Lee Hall, inspired by a book by William Feaver.** Based on the triumphant true story, a group of British miners discover a new way to express themselves and unexpectedly become art-world sensations. "Excitingly ambiguous, in-the-moment theater." –*NY Times.* "Heartfelt, moving and deeply politicized." –*Chicago Tribune.* [5M, 2W] ISBN: 978-0-8222-2507-2

★ **RELATIVELY SPEAKING by Ethan Coen, Elaine May and Woody Allen.** In TALKING CURE, Ethan Coen uncovers the sort of insanity that can only come from family. Elaine May explores the hilarity of passing in GEORGE IS DEAD. In HONEYMOON MOTEL, Woody Allen invites you to the sort of wedding day you won't forget. "Firecracker funny." –*NY Times.* "A rollicking good time." –*New Yorker.* [8M, 7W] ISBN: 978-0-8222-2394-8

★ **SONS OF THE PROPHET by Stephen Karam.** If to live is to suffer, then Joseph Douaihy is more alive than most. With unexplained chronic pain and the fate of his reeling family on his shoulders, Joseph's health, sanity, and insurance premium are on the line. "Explosively funny." –*NY Times.* "At once deep, deft and beautifully made." –*New Yorker.* [5M, 3W] ISBN: 978-0-8222-2597-3

★ **THE MOUNTAINTOP by Katori Hall.** A gripping reimagination of events the night before the assassination of the civil rights leader Dr. Martin Luther King, Jr. "An ominous electricity crackles through the opening moments." –*NY Times.* "[A] thrilling, wild, provocative flight of magical realism." –*Associated Press.* "Crackles with theatricality and a humanity more moving than sainthood." –*NY Newsday.* [1M, 1W] ISBN: 978-0-8222-2603-1

★ **ALL NEW PEOPLE by Zach Braff.** Charlie is 35, heartbroken, and just wants some time away from the rest of the world. Long Beach Island seems to be the perfect escape until his solitude is interrupted by a motley parade of misfits who show up and change his plans. "Consistently and sometimes sensationally funny." –*NY Times.* "A morbidly funny play about the trendy new existential condition of being young, adorable, and miserable." –*Variety.* [2M, 2W] ISBN: 978-0-8222-2562-1

DRAMATISTS PLAY SERVICE, INC.
440 Park Avenue South, New York, NY 10016 212-683-8960 Fax 212-213-1539
postmaster@dramatists.com www.dramatists.com

NEW PLAYS

★ **CLYBOURNE PARK by Bruce Norris.** WINNER OF THE 2011 PULITZER PRIZE AND 2012 TONY AWARD. Act One takes place in 1959 as community leaders try to stop the sale of a home to a black family. Act Two is set in the same house in the present day as the now predominantly African-American neighborhood battles to hold its ground. "Vital, sharp-witted and ferociously smart." –*NY Times.* "A theatrical treasure…Indisputably, uproariously funny." –*Entertainment Weekly.* [4M, 3W] ISBN: 978-0-8222-2697-0

★ **WATER BY THE SPOONFUL by Quiara Alegría Hudes.** WINNER OF THE 2012 PULITZER PRIZE. A Puerto Rican veteran is surrounded by the North Philadelphia demons he tried to escape in the service. "This is a very funny, warm, and yes uplifting play." –*Hartford Courant.* "The play is a combination poem, prayer and app on how to cope in an age of uncertainty, speed and chaos." –*Variety.* [4M, 3W] ISBN: 978-0-8222-2716-8

★ **RED by John Logan.** WINNER OF THE 2010 TONY AWARD. Mark Rothko has just landed the biggest commission in the history of modern art. But when his young assistant, Ken, gains the confidence to challenge him, Rothko faces the agonizing possibility that his crowning achievement could also become his undoing. "Intense and exciting." –*NY Times.* "Smart, eloquent entertainment." –*New Yorker.* [2M] ISBN: 978-0-8222-2483-9

★ **VENUS IN FUR by David Ives.** Thomas, a beleaguered playwright/director, is desperate to find an actress to play Vanda, the female lead in his adaptation of the classic sadomasochistic tale *Venus in Fur.* "Ninety minutes of good, kinky fun." –*NY Times.* "A fast-paced journey into one man's entrapment by a clever, vengeful female." –*Associated Press.* [1M, 1W] ISBN: 978-0-8222-2603-1

★ **OTHER DESERT CITIES by Jon Robin Baitz.** Brooke returns home to Palm Springs after a six-year absence and announces that she is about to publish a memoir dredging up a pivotal and tragic event in the family's history—a wound they don't want reopened. "Leaves you feeling both moved and gratifyingly sated." –*NY Times.* "A genuine pleasure." –*NY Post.* [2M, 3W] ISBN: 978-0-8222-2605-5

★ **TRIBES by Nina Raine.** Billy was born deaf into a hearing family and adapts brilliantly to his family's unconventional ways, but it's not until he meets Sylvia, a young woman on the brink of deafness, that he finally understands what it means to be understood. "A smart, lively play." –*NY Times.* "[A] bright and boldly provocative drama." –*Associated Press.* [3M, 2W] ISBN: 978-0-8222-2751-9

DRAMATISTS PLAY SERVICE, INC.
440 Park Avenue South, New York, NY 10016 212-683-8960 Fax 212-213-1539
postmaster@dramatists.com www.dramatists.com